Original title:
The Hidden Path

Copyright © 2024 Creative Arts Management OÜ
All rights reserved.

Author: Isaac Ravenscroft
ISBN HARDBACK: 978-9916-90-042-0
ISBN PAPERBACK: 978-9916-90-043-7

The Call of Ancestral Echoes

In twilight's embrace, the whispers flow,
From ages past, where shadows grow.
Through ancient woods, their voices rise,
A chorus soft beneath the skies.

Beneath the stars, old tales are spun,
Of battles lost and victories won.
Each heartbeat drums with history's might,
Echoing truths in the still of night.

With every breeze, a story shared,
Of dreams once dreamt and souls that dared.
The roots run deep, the ties are strong,
Ancestral echoes, a timeless song.

Awake my spirit, heed the call,
From distant lands where shadows fall.
At every crossroads, wisdom waits,
To guide us through life's twisted fates.

Journey Through the Unseen

Beneath the cloak of twilight's glow,
Whispers of paths, we long to know.
Stars peer through veils of misty dreams,
Guiding us forth with silent beams.

Each step we take, a moment rare,
In shadows deep, we find our care.
The heart beats strong, a compass true,
In the journey's depths, we start anew.

Footprints on Silent Ground

In quiet woods where echoes play,
Footprints linger, fade away.
Nature's breath holds secrets bold,
Stories of journeys yet untold.

Leaf and stone, the earth's own sound,
Each step we leave, a bond profound.
Among the trees, in whispers found,
We trace our lives on silent ground.

Echoes of an Untrodden Way

Through valleys deep, in twilight's arc,
We wander forth, igniting spark.
Voices of dreams on the wind do sing,
Guiding the heart to embrace the spring.

Paths untraveled, spirits free,
Holding the truth of what can be.
In every echo, a chance to sway,
To find ourselves on an untrodden way.

Veils of the Unexplored

In realms where light and shadow blend,
Veils of mystery do extend.
With curious hearts, we seek the hue,
Of hidden worlds that feel so new.

Unseen horizons call our name,
Daring us to join the game.
With every step, we lift the shroud,
Embracing wonders, fierce and proud.

Unseen Vistas of Heartfelt Horizons

In shadows cast by dreams we chase,
New paths emerge, a warm embrace.
Each step reveals a hidden light,
Unseen vistas call through the night.

Moments linger, time stands still,
Hearts awakened, breaths fulfill.
Horizons break, like dawn's sweet song,
Where we belong, where we are strong.

Together, we traverse the skies,
A tapestry where love replies.
Uncharted lands of tender grace,
Hearts aligned in sacred space.

Finding Clarity in the Fog

Amidst the haze, a whisper flows,
Through veils of mist, a light bestows.
We seek the truth in every sigh,
Finding clarity as shadows fly.

With gentle steps, we push ahead,
Through tangled thoughts our hearts are led.
The fog begins to ebb away,
Revealing dreams that greet the day.

As echoes fade, we find our way,
With clarity, our spirits sway.
In every heartbeat, hope remains,
Through fog and fear, love breaks the chains.

Whispers of Nostalgia in the Breeze

Soft echoes dance on evening air,
A whisper flows, a tender care.
Nostalgia paints with warm embrace,
Old memories linger, time and space.

Beneath the trees, where shadows fall,
The breeze recalls our laughter's call.
In every gust, a story told,
Of moments cherished, hearts of gold.

As twilight falls, the world slows down,
In whispers of the past, we're found.
In every sigh, a secret shared,
With nostalgia's touch, we are prepared.

Trails of Dust and Wonder

On dusty trails where footsteps lie,
Adventure calls beneath the sky.
With every turn, new sights unfold,
In trails of dust, our dreams are told.

The earth beneath our wanderlust,
Each grain a promise, each step a trust.
Through winding paths of wild delight,
We chase the stars that gleam at night.

With every breath, the world expands,
In trails of dust, together we stand.
Wonder leads us through the unknown,
With hearts ablaze, we've truly grown.

Murmurs of the Overlooked Route

Whispers dance upon the breeze,
Shadows linger 'neath the trees.
Footprints lost to time and space,
Silent paths, a hidden grace.

Rustling leaves tell quiet tales,
Of journeys missed and forgotten trails.
Gentle calls from nature's heart,
Guide the seeker to depart.

Steps into the Abyss

Echoes tremble in the dark,
Each step forward leaves a mark.
Eyes closed tight, a breath held deep,
Into the void, where secrets sleep.

Time stands still within the black,
No turning back, no light to track.
Fingers stretch to grasp the night,
In the abyss, fears ignite.

Trails of the Unfamiliar

Winding roads of tangled dreams,
Where sunlight breaks in fractured beams.
Every turn, a chance to find,
The stories left within the mind.

Footsteps echo on the ground,
In spaces where new hopes are found.
With open hearts and eyes so wide,
We venture forth, our fears aside.

Beyond the Visible Horizon

Colors blend at twilight's call,
The sky embraces one and all.
Paths unseen stretch far and wide,
Beyond the reach of thought and pride.

Stars awaken in the night,
Guiding souls with gentle light.
Infinite realms await the brave,
Beyond horizons, dreams will save.

The Unseen Compass

In shadows deep, we often roam,
With hearts that yearn to find their home.
A silent guide, the compass glows,
Through tangled paths, its wisdom flows.

Each step we take, a choice to make,
The unseen thread, no fear we stake.
With every twist, our fates entwined,
The compass leads, our hearts aligned.

Mystic Turns of Fate

In twilight's hush, the fates conspire,
With whispered secrets, a hidden fire.
The winding road, a tale unfolds,
Of mysteries woven, of heroes bold.

With every turn, the dice are cast,
In shadows linger tales of the past.
A dance of chance, a fateful tie,
In mystic realms, we soar and fly.

Whispers of the Veiled Way

Through silence deep, the whispers call,
A hidden path where shadows fall.
The veiled way leads, a gentle guide,
To places where our dreams abide.

In secret glades, where time stands still,
The heart does speak, the spirit will.
With every step, we come alive,
In whispered dreams, we learn to thrive.

Secrets Beneath the Canopy

Beneath the leaves, where stories sleep,
The ancient roots in silence keep.
A tapestry of life unfolds,
With secrets rich, and wonders bold.

The whispers dance on breezes light,
In shadows cast, the tales ignite.
A hidden world of magic thrives,
Where nature's pulse forever drives.

Secrets in the Underbrush

Whispers dance among the leaves,
Hidden tales that gently weave.
Shadows shift beneath the boughs,
Nature's secrets, silent vows.

Every rustle tells a story,
Of forgotten paths and glory.
In the twilight's tender hush,
Life exudes a sacred rush.

Beneath the moss, the stories thrive,
Old and new, they come alive.
In the thicket, dreams converge,
From the stillness, hopes emerge.

Let us wander, hearts anew,
Through the greens, where secrets brew.
In the underbrush we find,
Treasures waiting, intertwined.

The Soft Call of Distant Echoes

Across the hills, a sound does rise,
Whispers carried through the skies.
A melody of times long past,
Echoes lingering, deep and vast.

In the distance, voices play,
Flowing gently, night and day.
Hearts can feel their distant pull,
In the silence, memories lull.

Footsteps trace the ancient ground,
Lost in reverie, peace is found.
Each soft call a guiding light,
Leading us through the velvet night.

Awaiting dreams beyond the veil,
In these echoes, hearts set sail.
Through the currents, souls will glide,
On the soft call, we confide.

Beyond the Well-Hidden Gates

Where the ivy twists and twines,
Ancient stones hold whispered signs.
Beyond the gates, a realm awaits,
Mysteries dwell, and magic fates.

With every step, the air feels thick,
Secrets thrum, the heart beats quick.
Hidden wonders beckon all,
In the shadows, siren's call.

Each rusted hinge creaks a tale,
Of forgotten paths, a hidden trail.
Beyond the gates, adventure sings,
In the air, the promise clings.

Shall we venture, break the chain?
To seek the joy beyond the pain?
Through well-hidden gates we roam,
Finding in the unknown, a home.

The Serpent's Secret Course

In the grass, a serpent glides,
Through the brush where silence hides.
With a flick, it charts its way,
In the shadows, where it may.

Curves and bends, a delicate dance,
In the wild, a fleeting chance.
Secrets swirl within its path,
Embodying nature's wrath.

Beneath the leaves, it softly sighs,
Dreaming of the open skies.
In stillness, it finds its home,
A world of wonder, free to roam.

As it whispers to the night,
Underneath the silver light.
The serpent knows the hidden way,
Guiding hearts to seize the day.

Whispers Beneath the Canopy

The leaves above softly sway,
In a breeze that sings the day.
Nature's voice, a gentle light,
Whispers secrets, pure delight.

Shadows dance upon the ground,
In this magic, lost, yet found.
Underneath the heavy boughs,
I hear hope, I hear vows.

Birds chirp sweetly, a soft tune,
Their calls echo 'neath the moon.
Life unfolds in shades of green,
In this realm, a tranquil scene.

As I wander, time stands still,
Nature's heart, a soothing thrill.
With every step, I feel alive,
In this haven, I can thrive.

Shadows of a Forgotten Trail

Along the path where memories dwell,
Echoes linger, they weave and swell.
Footprints faded in the dirt,
Tell stories of joy and hurt.

The trees stand tall, wise and old,
Guarding secrets, brave and bold.
Beneath their shade, the past unfolds,
Whispered tales that heart beholds.

Dappled sunlight breaks the gloom,
Life within the shadows bloom.
Each step forward, time is bound,
In twilight's touch, lost voices sound.

Nature keeps its ancient lore,
Each moment rich, forever more.
In this sanctuary of the past,
I find a peace that's meant to last.

Secrets Woven in Twilight

As dusk descends, colors blend,
The day retreats, night's hand extends.
Stars awaken, shy and bright,
Guardians of the coming night.

Whispers float on evening air,
Softly weaving tales laid bare.
In the stillness, shadows sigh,
Secrets held as time slips by.

Moonlight bathes the world in grace,
A silver touch, a warm embrace.
In this hour, dreams take flight,
Carried gently on the night.

With every heartbeat, stories call,
In twilight's arms, I feel it all.
Life's fleeting moments, bittersweet,
Alchemy of dreams and heartbeats.

Beneath the Leafy Veil

Nestled under emerald leaves,
Where the heart of nature weaves.
A tapestry of light and shade,
Here, my fears begin to fade.

Softly rustling, nature breathes,
Carrying whispers through the eaves.
In this sanctuary, I belong,
In perfect rhythm with the song.

Gentle breezes dance with grace,
Every moment, a warm embrace.
Beneath the veil, dreams intertwine,
In this haven, love will shine.

As I wander through the tree,
Nature's spirit speaks to me.
Life unfolds, a sacred tale,
In the magic of the leafy veil.

Navigating the Unspoken

Silence holds a thousand truths,
Words hang heavy in the air.
Between each glance, a story waits,
A language found in heart and stare.

Echoes linger in the dark,
Thoughts that drift like autumn leaves.
Bridges built on whispered sighs,
What remains is all that believes.

Yet moments speak without a sound,
As feelings weave a silent thread.
In the shadows, meaning grows,
Navigating what's left unsaid.

A gentle nod, a fleeting smile,
In the stillness, we connect.
Through the unvoiced, we can learn,
Our hearts find paths we can reflect.

Beneath the Shroud of Leaves

In the forest of green whispers,
Nature wraps us in its quilt.
Sunlight dances through the branches,
Time stands still, our worries built.

The rustle speaks of hidden things,
Stories etched in bark and stone.
Birdsong weaves a gentle spell,
Beneath the shroud, we are not alone.

Roots intertwine beneath our feet,
Life thrives in shadows thick and deep.
Secrets sleep in every nook,
While ancient wisdom softly keeps.

We wander, lost yet fully found,
In this haven, hearts align.
Beneath the leaves, we breathe as one,
Nature's rhythm, pure and fine.

The Quiet Quest

In moments stripped of worldly clamor,
A journey sprouts within the soul.
With each step, a question lingers,
What do we seek? What makes us whole?

Winds carry thoughts like feathers light,
The path unfolds in twilight's glow.
With every breath, we glean our vision,
The quiet whispers help us know.

Mountains rise, rivers twist and turn,
Lessons echo through the space.
Through silence, clarity emerges,
In stillness, we uncover grace.

The quest reveals the heart's own map,
Where courage blooms and doubts subside.
In the quiet, we find our truth,
A treasure held where dreams abide.

Through the Gossamer Haze

Morning breaks with soft caress,
Mist hangs low like a lover's sigh.
Chasing shadows, hearts will dance,
Through gossamer, we learn to fly.

Each step shimmers on the dew,
A world reborn in muted light.
Fleeting moments stitch together,
Dreams that pulse, both bold and bright.

Whispers echo on the breeze,
Carrying hopes, both new and old.
Through the haze, we find our way,
A tapestry of warm and cold.

With every heartbeat, we explore,
The fragile beauty life can be.
Through gossamer, veils unveil,
A journey defined by what we see.

The Untold Stories of Winding Ways

Paths curve under the ancient trees,
Whispers carried on the gentle breeze.
Footprints lead to places unknown,
Secrets held in the roots and stone.

Each twist reveals a faded rhyme,
Echoes of forgotten time.
Stories etched in silence bold,
Winding tales yet to be told.

In shadows dance the memories bright,
Guiding us through the shrouded night.
With every turn, the journey grows,
In winding ways, the mystery flows.

Beneath the stars, the stories mix,
Life and fate weave through the tricks.
The untold speaks with every sway,
In the heart of the winding way.

Through the Veil of Time

Moments hang like mist on dawn,
Fragile threads of time are drawn.
Whispers from the ages blend,
In the silence, the echoes mend.

Each heartbeat marks a fleeting trace,
Of love and loss in endless space.
Glimmers of the past arise,
Through the veil where memory lies.

Shadows flicker, soft and pale,
Stories woven in the veil.
Time's tapestry, rich and vast,
In every stitch, we find the past.

Through the veil, we dare to roam,
Seeking distant lands called home.
Moments lost, reclaimed in rhyme,
As we journey through the veil of time.

Ghosts of Past Wanderers

Wandering souls in twilight's glow,
Faintly seen, they come and go.
Echoes call from ages grey,
Ghostly whispers in the fray.

With every footstep soft and clear,
The past returns, we feel it near.
Haunting tales from ages past,
In the shadows, memories cast.

They linger where the shadows play,
Memories from a distant day.
In silence, their stories weave,
Of love and loss that never leave.

Ghostly wanderers, lost yet found,
In their presence, truth unbound.
Through the corridors of time they roam,
The ghosts of wanderers seek their home.

Labyrinths of the Mind

In the depths where thoughts collide,
Labyrinths twist, and fears abide.
Winding paths of hope and dread,
In silence, countless secrets spread.

Each corner hides a flickering light,
Questions linger, taking flight.
Truth and doubt in shadows blend,
In the maze where visions bend.

The heart maps out a winding plot,
Seeking solace in every thought.
In the corridors, we often find,
The labyrinths of the restless mind.

Through twists and turns, we chase our fate,
The echoes of dreams resonate.
In the tangled web, we seek to see,
The labyrinths of who we might be.

Discoveries in the Dappled Shadows

Beneath the trees where whispers dwell,
I found a world, a secret spell.
Sunbeams dance on leaves so bright,
Guiding me through fading light.

Every step reveals a clue,
A hidden path, a morning dew.
Colors blend, a playful game,
Nature's art, it calls my name.

In silence, stories softly shared,
With every breath, my heart is bared.
Life unfolds in quiet grace,
In dappled shadows, I find my place.

Moments linger, time stands still,
As I embrace the love I feel.
Discoveries bloom with every sigh,
In this lush world, I learn to fly.

Footsteps on the Faintly Lit Trail

Where moonlight meets the winding way,
I tread softly at the end of day.
Footsteps echo, a gentle sound,
In nature's arms, I'm tightly bound.

The path is marked by secrets old,
With tales of warmth and legends told.
Each twist and turn a song unsung,
In twilight's grasp, my spirit's wrung.

The air is cool, the night is shy,
Stars peek out from the velvet sky.
I wander onward, heart aglow,
Through shadows deep, I long to go.

With every step, I learn to trust,
In whispered winds and ancient dust.
The trail may fade, but I remain,
Forever changed by the journey's gain.

When Stars Align in Subtle Silence

In quiet nights, the cosmos sighs,
A tapestry of endless skies.
Stars align in gentle grace,
Illuminating our secret space.

Beneath this vast and twinkling sea,
Whispers of fate beckon to me.
Moments pause, the world feels right,
In subtle silence, a guiding light.

Hearts synchronize with the celestial dance,
Finding joy in a fleeting glance.
Time stands still, a magic spun,
When stars align, two hearts are one.

Dreams unfold like petals bright,
In the calm embrace of night.
Eternal truths revealed in starlight,
In subtle silence, love takes flight.

Through the Eyes of the Overlooked

In shadows cast, a story waits,
A tale of life through hidden gates.
Eyes that wander, souls confined,
In every heart, a love designed.

The overlooked, the ones ignored,
Hold visions that can not be stored.
Through cracked facades and whispered dreams,
A world unfolds in silent themes.

With gentle grace, they paint their art,
Each brushstroke born from aching heart.
In every glance, a universe,
A beauty rare, diverse, and terse.

In every voice, a truth untold,
The strength of shadows, brave and bold.
Through the eyes of those passed by,
We find the spark that lights the sky.

Echoes Lost Among the Pines

Whispers float through ancient trees,
Dancing gently on the breeze.
Footsteps linger from days of yore,
Echoes call from a distant shore.

Mossy carpets, soft and green,
Hiding secrets, rarely seen.
Pinecones fall with a quiet grace,
Nature's touch, a warm embrace.

Sunlight dapples the forest floor,
Inviting souls to explore.
The scent of earth and fading light,
Guiding wanderers through the night.

In time, we'll join the whispered song,
Where reverent hearts have belonged.
Beneath the boughs, so strong and wise,
We'll find the peace that never dies.

The Dance of Light and Shadow

Sunrise spills across the land,
Brushes gold with a gentle hand.
Shadows stretch and intertwine,
In a ballet, divine design.

Leaves shimmer in the morning hue,
As light ignites a vibrant view.
Each flutter casts a fleeting trace,
A whisper in this sacred space.

Twilight dims, the colors fade,
Darkness wraps the world it made.
Yet even then, the stars will gleam,
In the night's soft, tranquil dream.

The dance continues, day to night,
In every flicker, pure delight.
For in this rhythm, we all find,
A harmony that loves mankind.

Inhabiting the Quiet Ruins

Crumbled walls stand proud and tall,
Telling tales of a time gone small.
Vines embrace the stony grace,
Nature's touch in this sacred place.

Whispers echo through the stone,
A harmony for those alone.
Lost laughter in the empty halls,
History's breath in fleeting calls.

Moss and ivy, time's embrace,
Weaving threads in this still space.
With every shadow, a story thrives,
In these ruins, memory survives.

As dusk descends, the silence reigns,
Cries of the past like soft, sweet chains.
Inhabiting these hallowed grounds,
The heart of history resounds.

Paths of Serendipity

Winding trails beneath the trees,
Whispers carried on the breeze.
Every step, a chance to find,
Glimmers of fate intertwined.

Serene moments, softly shared,
Serendipity, gently bared.
Unexpected turns bring delight,
In hidden paths, beyond the light.

Stars arrive to bless the night,
Guiding souls with twinkling light.
Together, we wander, hand in hand,
Exploring dreams across the land.

With each corner, a secret glows,
Showcasing where true magic flows.
Paths of joy on this journey vast,
Leading us into adventures cast.

Echoes of Forgotten Steps

In the hush of twilight's glow,
Ghosts of laughter dance below,
Whispers tracing paths of time,
Memories held in rhythm and rhyme.

Footfalls soft on dusty roads,
Storytellers in faded codes,
Each stone tells of love and loss,
Upon the trail of dreams we cross.

With echoes deep in the night air,
Candles flicker, spirits share,
The tales of those who came before,
Their shadows linger evermore.

Through the silence, a heartbeat plays,
A melody of yesterdays,
In every step, a story stirs,
In the wind, the past prefers.

Uncharted Territories of the Heart

Maps lie folded, edges worn,
In a world where hope is born,
Stars above, a guiding light,
Leading dreams into the night.

Paths untraveled, wild and free,
Whispers call to you and me,
Through the forests thick and deep,
Where secrets of the heart still sleep.

Adventures wait in every glance,
A twinkle, then a daring dance,
With every leap, we break the mold,
In love's embrace, we find the bold.

Unseen roads stretch far and wide,
On this journey, hearts abide,
Through uncharted lands we roam,
In each other's arms, we find home.

Fragments of a Silent Journey

In shadows cast by silent trees,
Whispers ride the evening breeze,
A solitary path unfolds,
Stories wrapped in quiet holds.

Footsteps soft on ancient ground,
In the stillness, truths are found,
Every glance, a piece of art,
Fragments stitched into the heart.

Memories in gentle sighs,
Hidden 'neath the endless skies,
A canvas painted, life portrayed,
In solitude, our fears allayed.

Through the stillness, we explore,
In every silence, so much more,
Fragments come together whole,
On this journey, we find our role.

Where Footprints Fade

On the shore where waves embrace,
Echoes linger, time's soft trace,
Footprints in the sand are laid,
Yet with the tide, they quickly fade.

Moments slip through fingers tight,
Like shadows lost to fleeting light,
In the ebb and flow of days,
We lose ourselves in sunlit haze.

Yet every step leaves something true,
In the hearts of me and you,
Though pathways may grow dim and worn,
In love's bright spark, we are reborn.

When footprints fade, we carry on,
In the memories that are drawn,
For in the transient, we find grace,
A journey shared, time's sweet embrace.

The Unraveled Journey of Self

Each step reveals a hidden truth,
Awakens dreams buried in youth.
Shadows whisper in the night,
Guiding souls to find their light.

Paths once tangled start to clear,
Voices echo, soft and near.
Fragile hearts begin to mend,
In this journey, we transcend.

Mountains rise and valleys fall,
Lessons learned through it all.
With every twist, we find our way,
In the dance of night and day.

To know oneself is pure delight,
In shadows deep, we reach for light.
The journey long, yet richly blessed,
In every trial, we find our quest.

Hints of Light in the Abyss

In the depths where silence dwells,
Echoes murmur, whisper spells.
Flickers shine from far away,
Guiding hearts that drift astray.

The darkness calls, it pulls, it bends,
Yet hope persists, it never ends.
Even shadows bear their grace,
Hints of light in a solemn place.

Doubt may seep like creeping vines,
Yet resilience within us shines.
Through the void, we learn to fight,
Finding strength in sorrow's plight.

Each glimmer is a gentle nudge,
In the abyss, love will not budge.
From the dark, we rise anew,
Hints of light, forever true.

The Corners of Imagination

In quiet corners, thoughts take flight,
Colors mingle, pure delight.
Dreams unfold in written lines,
Where every heart and mind entwines.

A canvas broad, both bold and vast,
In each moment, shadows cast.
Whispers dance on melodies,
In the air, creativity frees.

Visions stir like waves of art,
From the depths, we find our part.
In the labyrinth of our minds,
Endless wonders, truth unwinds.

In these corners, fear recedes,
Imagination plants its seeds.
Let us wander, let us play,
In this realm, we find our way.

Ascent to the Unknown Peaks

With courage strong, we climb the heights,
Chasing dawn, embracing nights.
Each step a story, each breath a song,
In the unknown, we feel we belong.

Rugged paths beneath our shoes,
Nature sings, we cannot lose.
The view reveals what lies ahead,
Dreams uncharted, hearts widespread.

Above the clouds, the air grows thin,
Yet every fail leads to a win.
In the summit's arms, we find our peace,
A quiet moment, a sweet release.

As we stand on this lofty brink,
The world below makes us rethink.
With open hearts, we face the skies,
The unknown peaks, where courage lies.

Lanterns in the Gloom

Flickers cast shadows deep,
Whispers of secrets we keep.
Glow through the night, serene,
Guiding us to moments unseen.

In the dark, they softly hum,
Echoes of a distant drum.
We tread on paths lit by dreams,
Shimmering like silver streams.

Beneath the stars, we find our way,
Chasing the night, till break of day.
With lanterns held high, we roam,
Finding our lost pieces, our home.

The Mysterious Footfalls

In the silence, footsteps glide,
Secrets hidden deep inside.
Who walks where shadows dwell?
Can you hear the echoes swell?

Crimson leaves whisper and sigh,
As the whispers drift and fly.
In the night, a cloaked figure,
Under the moon's watchful rigor.

Each footfall tells a tale,
Of journeys that twist and pale.
Mysteries woven in the dark,
Leaving behind a solemn mark.

In Pursuit of Unwritten Stories

Pages blank, a pen in hand,
Dreams flutter like grains of sand.
Each stroke a whisper, a wish,
Awaiting the words to embellish.

Hidden tales of love and woes,
In every heart where passion grows.
We chase the ink through time's embrace,
Hoping to find our rightful place.

With every line, a world takes flight,
Illuminated by purest light.
In the quest for tales untold,
We pen our dreams, both brave and bold.

Through the Kaleidoscope of Color

Vibrant hues swirl and blend,
A tapestry with no end.
Through patterns that dance and sway,
Life's adventures on display.

Petals of crimson, leaves of gold,
With stories vibrant and bold.
Sunsets bleed into the night,
A kaleidoscope of pure delight.

Each color tells a tale anew,
Of past and present, whispers true.
In every shade, a memory gleams,
Reflecting our wildest dreams.

Midnight's Silent Detour

Beneath the stars, the shadows creep,
Whispers of night, secrets they keep.
Silent footsteps on a winding lane,
Lost in tranquility, free from pain.

Moonlight dances on the cool, wet grass,
Time slows down, as moments pass.
In the stillness, a heartbeats sound,
In midnight's arms, solace is found.

The Trail Less Illuminated

Paths overgrown, hidden from sight,
Leading the wanderer into the night.
Leaves rustle softly, a beckoning call,
Journey begins where most will not crawl.

Faint whispers echo through the thick trees,
Secrets entwined within the gentle breeze.
With every step, a story unfolds,
In the shadows, the truth just molds.

Lost in the Underbrush

Tangled branches clutch the way,
Nature's embrace makes one sway.
A labyrinth of green where dreams collide,
Within each corner, unknown things hide.

Muffled sounds of the world outside,
In the underbrush, the spirits bide.
Time feels lost; reality's gone,
Among the thickets, I wander on.

Pathways of the Unnoticed

Faded trails where few have tread,
Stories linger, though words are dead.
Silent echoes of those who roam,
In spaces between, they call it home.

Every forgotten route we find,
Bears the mark of the wandering kind.
Paths that twist and deliberately turn,
Hold the wisdom for which we yearn.

The Enigma of Ashen Treads

In shadows dance the whispered trails,
Forgotten paths where silence pales.
The echoes of what once was grand,
Now buried deep in ashen sand.

Flickering lights of distant dreams,
Fade softly into muted screams.
Each tread a story left untold,
In the shrouded mist, the memories fold.

Curved pathways twist like ancient lore,
Leading the heart to seek for more.
Yet every step, a fleeting wish,
A shadow flutters, a ghostly fish.

But in the ash, the truth remains,
In hushed corners, love still reigns.
Embrace the enigma, let it flow,
For ash can nurture seeds to grow.

Lanterns Leading Astray

Beneath the night, the lanterns glow,
With promises they softly throw.
Yet every flicker leads to doubt,
Whispers of what it's all about.

They guide the lost with gentle light,
While casting shadows deep as night.
Each path infused with dreams once bright,
Now tangled in the fading sight.

The wandering souls, they chase the flame,
In hopes to find a missing name.
But every turn grows dimmer still,
As lanterns wane against their will.

So tread with care, though lights entice,
For not all paths lead to paradise.
Within their glow, a lesson true,
Sometimes the false can seem like new.

Silhouettes of Lost Aspirations

In the twilight, dreams take flight,
Silhouettes dance, lost from sight.
Each figure woven, a life once bright,
Now shadows linger in the night.

With every pulse, the echoes sigh,
Of visions cast beneath the sky.
Chasing whispers of what could be,
Yet bound by chains we cannot see.

The canvas blurred with hopes and fears,
Each stroke eroded by the years.
Yet still, they haunt the quiet air,
Silhouettes whispering, unaware.

But within the mirage, a spark remains,
Flashes of joy amidst the pains.
From shadows born, new dreams may rise,
In the heart's cradle, life never dies.

Threads of Fate Woven Softly

In the loom of life, the threads entwine,
Weaving stories both yours and mine.
In twilight's hush, the fibers sigh,
Binding destinies that may fly.

Each strand a moment, a choice defined,
Woven gently, yet sharply aligned.
As needles pierce through hopes laid bare,
They stitch the hopes with tender care.

The tapestry glimmers with colors bold,
In faded hues of dreams retold.
Every knot a lesson to abide,
Holding wisdom where love resides.

So let the fibers tell their tale,
Of joy and sorrow, of winds that wail.
For in this art, we find the key,
To unlock the truth of you and me.

Entwined in Nature's Embrace

In the whispering woods, dreams take flight,
Beneath the canopy, soft and light.
Leaves dance gently, a tender song,
Nature's embrace where we belong.

Rivers murmur secrets of time,
Mountains stand tall, pure and sublime.
The sun spills gold on emerald green,
In this stillness, our hearts convene.

Flora blooms in a vibrant array,
Colors bursting, chasing gray.
Each petal, a story waiting to tell,
In nature's realm, we weave our spell.

As twilight falls, the shadows play,
Stars emerge to light our way.
Entwined in nature, we find our grace,
In the wild's heart, a sacred space.

Pathways of the Soul's Desire

Every step taken, a choice defined,
We walk through shadows, our souls aligned.
Footpaths winding, secrets unfold,
In silence, our stories are told.

Desires linger like stars in the night,
Guiding our journey, a flickering light.
With each turn, new visions arise,
In the depths of our hearts, the soul's surprise.

Through valleys deep and mountains high,
Whispers of longing rustle the sky.
We chase horizons, forever we seek,
In pathways of dreams, we find our peak.

Every heartbeat echoes the quest,
For what we yearn, for what is best.
In this odyssey, we aim to inspire,
Through pathways forged by the soul's desire.

The Veiled Voyage

Across the ocean, mist hides the dawn,
A vessel sails where the light is drawn.
Waves embrace the hull with a sigh,
As secrets beckon from the deep blue sky.

The horizon blurs in a dance of fate,
A compass spins, we navigate.
In every gust, memories swirl,
Tales of wonder begin to unfurl.

Stars above like lanterns glow,
Guiding the way through the ebb and flow.
With hearts as anchors, we drift and roam,
In the veiled voyage, we find our home.

Mysteries whisper in the cool night air,
Each wave carries a dream to share.
As the journey unfolds, we embrace the tide,
In this veiled adventure, we reside.

Footfalls of Forgotten Dreams

In the echo of steps, memories sway,
Footfalls linger, marking the way.
Whispers of dreams long left behind,
In shadows remembered, solace we find.

A path paved with hopes and tears,
Carried through time, echoing years.
With every heartbeat, we retrace,
The footprints of dreams that still embrace.

Gazettes of joy, in sepia tones,
Map out the journey of heart and bones.
Yet in the silence, a call remains,
To uncover the joy in forgotten chains.

We walk with care through echoes of night,
Reviving the dreams that once took flight.
In the footfalls of time, let us glean,
The beauty still shines in what might have been.

Uncharted Windsong

Whispers ride on breezes light,
Through valleys deep and mountains high.
A melody of dreams takes flight,
In skies where hopes and shadows lie.

Each note a map of worlds unknown,
Where spirits dance and tales unfold.
On unmarked paths, the winds have blown,
A symphony of hearts so bold.

With every gust, a secret shared,
In echoes soft of laughter's grace.
Through songs of old, the future dared,
To intertwine in time and space.

So sail with me on songs untamed,
Let courage guide our wandering feet.
Together we shall be reclaimed,
In winds of change, our souls will meet.

The Wayward Whisper

A breath of air, a gentle sigh,
Secrets carried on the breeze.
With every word, the echoes lie,
In dreams that dance among the trees.

The softest tones of truth and doubt,
In quiet corners, shadows blend.
A path once lost, now found throughout,
The whispers lead, dear heart, descend.

Through tangled tales of what may be,
The wayward dreams begin to weave.
In silence speaks the soul's decree,
That hope endures, we must believe.

With every footfall softly made,
We wander where the heart can feel.
Amongst the doubts, a bright cascade,
Where whispers turn to truths revealed.

Hushed Directions of the Heart

In silence, longing softly sways,
Against the backdrop of the night.
A tender ache in subtle ways,
Guides lost souls toward the light.

With each heartbeat, stories trace,
The lines of fate in fragile ink.
A dance is born in soft embrace,
Where hearts converge and dreams now think.

In quiet moments, secrets dwell,
Directions written in the stars.
Through whispered hopes, we weave our spell,
As love unravels hidden bars.

So trust the compass deep inside,
And follow where the whispers lead.
For in the hush, our hearts abide,
In paths of love, our souls are freed.

The Secret Lanes of Time

In corners dim where shadows play,
The lanes of time weave tales untold.
With every step, we drift away,
Through memories both warm and cold.

The moments dance like flickering light,
As echoes of our laughter blend.
In secret places out of sight,
The past converges, never end.

Each footfall whispers soft goodbyes,
Yet threads of joy hold us in thrall.
As seasons shift, the heart complies,
In these lanes, we rise and fall.

So take my hand and wander forth,
Through every twist, each solemn chime.
Together we will map our worth,
In the secret lanes of time.

Unknown Horizons Underfoot

Beneath the sky, the earth unfolds,
Whispers of dreams in silence told.
Footprints trace where shadows play,
Unknown horizons call us away.

Each step a story, a chance to find,
Secrets buried, left behind.
Nature's canvas, vast and deep,
Awakens jaws of slumbering sleep.

In every crack, a tale of old,
Rich with promises, yet untold.
The world beneath, alive and bright,
Guides our hearts toward the light.

We wander forth, through grass and stone,
To meet the unknown, never alone.
With every breath, the future gleams,
Unknown horizons hold our dreams.

Ghostly Breezes of Longing

In twilight's hush, the whispers flow,
Ghostly breezes, soft and low.
Carrying thoughts, both near and far,
Memories entwined, like a distant star.

Echoes dance in the cool night air,
Cradling wishes, tender care.
Through shadowed paths, our spirits roam,
Seeking warmth, a place called home.

Timeless sighs in the rustling leaves,
Filling hearts with what one believes.
The essence of love, bittersweet,
In every breeze, our souls meet.

A longing deep, like a wistful song,
In the ghostly air, we all belong.
For every heart that yearns to see,
Is lifted high by the breeze, set free.

The Journey Beyond Ordinary Sight

Through valleys deep and mountains high,
We seek the truths that never die.
With every step, our spirits soar,
To realms of wonder, forevermore.

The mundane fades, a world unveiled,
In colors bright, our fears curtailed.
Beyond the sight of ordinary eyes,
Awaits the magic, the great surprise.

In whispered tales, the heart's delight,
Guided by stars in velvet night.
In each horizon, a path unknown,
The journey vast, our seeds are sown.

With open hearts, let dreams ignite,
The journey calls, beyond the light.
For those who wander, ever bold,
Shall find the treasures, worth more than gold.

Windows into the Wilderness

Peering through the trees so tall,
Windows open, nature's call.
Each glance reveals a life anew,
The wilderness speaks, inviting you.

A tapestry of greens and blues,
In every shade, a world to choose.
Through shimmering leaves, the stories flow,
Windows into realms where wild things grow.

From mountain peak to river bend,
The wilds awaken, invite a friend.
In every rustle, in every sound,
The pulse of nature can be found.

So step inside this vibrant sphere,
Where every moment is crystal clear.
Through these windows, our hearts ignite,
In the wilderness, lost in delight.

Songs of the Lost Wanderer

In shadows deep, the lost do tread,
Through whispers soft, where thoughts are led.
A path unknown, in twilight's gleam,
They chase the outline of a dream.

Beneath vast skies, the stars align,
With every step, a thread they twine.
The echoes call from distant shores,
Awakening hope, as silence roars.

With weary feet, they wander still,
In search of solace, strength, and will.
The world unfolds in shades of grey,
But in their hearts, the light won't sway.

A song unfolds within the night,
Of endless journeys, boundless flight.
For even lost, they find their way,
In songs that guide, come what may.

The Song of Unseen Streams

In hidden glades, where whispers play,
The unseen streams weave night and day.
They carry tales of time untold,
In currents warm, in waters cold.

Through tangled roots, their journey winds,
In secret paths, the heart often finds.
The gentle flow, a soft embrace,
Reviving dreams, a tranquil space.

Each ripple speaks, a soft refrain,
Of nature's truths, of joy and pain.
With every bend, a new sight greets,
As wisdom flows in quiet beats.

So listen close to what they sing,
The unseen streams in whispers bring.
For those who seek in silent streams,
Will find the essence of their dreams.

Parables of the Untraveled Way

In tales of old, where stories breath,
The untraveled paths lie beneath.
Each step a lesson, each turn a guide,
In parables where truths abide.

With lanterns bright, they seek the light,
Through every shadow, every night.
The road obscured, yet hearts hold fast,
To wisdom gained from journeys past.

In moments still, with silence sweet,
They ponder life, the joy and heat.
With open minds, they learn to see,
The beauty found in ways that be.

So walk the path, embrace the strife,
For in each trial lies the life.
The parables, they softly say,
Are guides to those who choose to sway.

Traversing the Silent Wilderness

In silent woods, where shadows loom,
The wilderness unfolds its bloom.
A call to hearts, so pure and wild,
In nature's grasp, the soul is beguiled.

With every step, the earth feels new,
The breeze, a hymn, the sky so blue.
Among the trees, the spirits speak,
In rustles soft, in whispers meek.

The mountains rise, a steadfast view,
In solitude, the heart breaks through.
For in the quiet, strength is found,
As echoes of the past resound.

To traverse thus, the wild expanse,
Is to embrace a silent dance.
For in the stillness, wisdom grows,
And through the wild, the heart that knows.

Beneath the Surface of Solitude

In quiet depths where shadows play,
A whisper calls the hours away.
Beneath the calm, a tempest swells,
In silence, only the heart retells.

The world outside, a distant hum,
In solitude, we learn to run.
With every breath, a chance to see,
The hidden truths that set us free.

Beneath the weight of longing sighs,
A flicker emerges in the skies.
In stillness, we find the grace,
To hold the void, to leave no trace.

Yet in this quiet, we must roam,
To seek the light that feels like home.
For in the depths of solitude,
New paths arise, fresh interlude.

The Lurking Light

In shadows deep where doubt takes root,
A flicker glints, a subtle truth.
Though darkness reigns, the heart ignites,
And guides the way through endless nights.

The lurking light, a beacon clear,
Whispers softly, "Do not fear."
Through twisted trails and heavy boughs,
It beckons forth, it gently vows.

Each step we take unveils a spark,
A path ahead through timid dark.
With open hearts, we chase the glow,
The lurking light will always show.

So trust the gleam in corners dim,
For even shadows dance on whim.
The lurking light, a constant friend,
Will guide us home till journey's end.

In Search of the Elusive Route

With maps in hand and dreams in tow,
We wander paths where wild winds blow.
Through tangled woods and valleys vast,
The elusive route, we seek at last.

Footsteps echo, time eludes,
Lost in thoughts, the mind renews.
With every twist, the heart will yearn,
For roads less traveled, we discern.

Each bend reveals a choice to make,
In search of truth, our souls awake.
The journey's long, yet joy abounds,
In each new sight, adventure found.

So let us chase the dawn's embrace,
With faithful friends at a steady pace.
In search of routes that feel so true,
We find ourselves; we start anew.

Paths Cloaked in Twilight

As day retreats and shadows blend,
The twilight whispers, lovers send.
With every step, the world transforms,
In twilight's grip, a magic swarms.

Each path unfolds with velvet grace,
Where dreams entwine in soft embrace.
In dusky hues, the heart ignites,
As mystery dances in the nights.

With lanterns dim, we stroll along,
The songs of dusk, a cherished throng.
Where ancient trees in silence stand,
And secrets bloom upon the land.

So take my hand in twilight's glow,
Together through the night we'll go.
For in these paths, our spirits soar,
Cloaked in twilight, we'll seek for more.

Beneath the Boughs of Memory

Whispers dance on gentle breeze,
Echoes of laughter, soft and clear.
Beneath the boughs, the heart finds ease,
Carving moments, ever near.

Sunlight filters through the shade,
Painting stories on the ground.
In this haven, dreams invade,
Memories in silence sound.

Each leaf a tale, each shadow deep,
Guardians of our yesterdays.
In this grove, we treasure keep,
All the hopes our hearts can raise.

Time stands still, a sacred pause,
In the cradle of the past.
Beneath the boughs, we find our cause,
Love and laughter, meant to last.

The Quiet Revolution of the Forgotten

In the silence, change will rise,
Voices lost, now find their sound.
From the shadows, hope will prize,
Beneath the surface, truth is found.

Hands once idle, now ignite,
Stirring dreams long held at bay.
In their grip, the spark of light,
Guides the heart to find its way.

Eyes that wander, seeking more,
Look for kinship in the night.
In the stillness, spirits soar,
Silent battles brought to light.

Seeds of courage, bravely sown,
In the earth where shadows fall.
The forgotten, now have grown,
In the quiet, they stand tall.

Strands of Time among the Leaves

Golden threads weave through the trees,
Binding moments, soft and sweet.
In the rustle, secrets tease,
Every whisper, time's heartbeat.

Branches cradle the shifting light,
Casting shadows, stories weave.
In this dance of day and night,
Past and present interleave.

The leaves, they shimmer with the past,
Echoing what time bestows.
In their fall, reflections cast,
Every season's tale bestows.

Dance with me among the boughs,
Feel the pulse of what has flown.
In this moment, share our vows,
In the strands of time, we've grown.

The Gentle Push of Adventure

With a whisper, dreams take flight,
Curiosity, a guiding star.
In the dawn, our hearts unite,
Chasing wonders, near and far.

Every step, a story told,
Every breath, a chance to feel.
In the journey, brave and bold,
Life reveals its vivid seal.

Mountains rise to greet our gaze,
Rivers sing beneath the sky.
In the wild, the spirit plays,
As we wander, time drifts by.

With a gentle push, we soar,
On the wings of thoughts unbound.
Adventure calls us, evermore,
In the world, true magic found.

Fractured Whispers of Origin

In shadows deep, the stories lie,
A tapestry of stars up high.
Fragments murmur through the night,
Lost echoes of an ancient flight.

Beneath the earth, the roots entwine,
A dance of time, a thread divine.
Whispers stir the silent air,
Unraveling secrets held with care.

Memory threads through tangled dreams,
Reflections glimmer like moonbeams.
Past and present softly weave,
In fractured tales, we believe.

Voices call from long ago,
Of hidden paths we yearn to know.
The genesis of life and fate,
Whispers weave, creating wait.

Myths Woven in the Weeds

In tangled thickets, legends grow,
Ancient stories twist and flow.
Roots of wisdom, leaves of lore,
In every shadow, tales explore.

The grass hums soft with voices low,
Of heroes brave and hearts aglow.
Woven myths in gentle breeze,
Nature's secrets hide with ease.

Beneath the sun's warm, golden gaze,
Myths of old dance through the haze.
Each petal holds a saga grand,
In every leaf, a guiding hand.

Such tales of wonder, wild and free,
Echo softly through the trees.
In the weeds, our dreams align,
A tapestry of the divine.

The Elusive Embrace of Nature's Grasp

In whispered winds, a gentle hug,
Nature wraps us, warm and snug.
Leaves of green and skies of blue,
In her arms, we find what's true.

Streams that flow with laughter bright,
Chasing shadows, chasing light.
Mountains stand as ancients wise,
Guardians under azure skies.

Every flower, a fleeting kiss,
In her embrace, we find our bliss.
Nature's pulse, a steady beat,
In every heartbeat, life is sweet.

Yet fleeting moments slip away,
Like grains of sand at close of day.
In her grasp, we dance and sway,
The elusive love we crave to stay.

Paths that Disappear

In twilight's glow, the paths unwind,
Trails obscure, by time defined.
Each step taken stirs the ground,
In silence, echoes yet resound.

Footprints fade as shadows rise,
Disappearing beneath the skies.
The journey whispers soft and clear,
Yet all we seek begins to veer.

For every road has its own end,
And bends away where dreams ascend.
Paths that twist like smoke in air,
Lead us somewhere, unaware.

Yet still we wander, hearts ablaze,
Through tangled foliage, we'll navigate.
Paths may vanish, but we still strive,
In searching for what keeps alive.

Journey Along the Untrodden Road

Beneath the sky so wide and blue,
I wander forth, a spirit true.
The path unwinds with every step,
Each turn a secret I have kept.

The whispers call, through trees and leaves,
With tales of hope that nature weaves.
Adventures wait, untold, unseen,
A world alive, where I have been.

I breathe the air, so fresh, so pure,
Embrace the wild, my heart's allure.
The journey's long, but I am brave,
Beyond the path, the soul's enclave.

At dusk I pause to feel the night,
The stars above, a guide, a light.
For every road, a tale is spun,
In shadows cast, my spirit's run.

Veils of Mist and Memory

In twilight's glow, the mist does rise,
A shroud of dreams 'neath silver skies.
With every breath, a whisper stirs,
The echoes of what once occurred.

Through veils of gray, the past unfolds,
With stories wrapped in threadbare folds.
Each memory a haunting song,
That calls to me, where I belong.

I wander through the foggy haze,
In search of lost and precious days.
The fleeting moments, soft and shy,
Like fleeting stars that wink and die.

Yet in this mist, the heart can see,
The paths that shape our history.
With every turn, the past will blend,
In veils of mist, we find our thread.

The Unseen Trail of Dreams

In shadows cast by moonlit beams,
I tread the path of silent dreams.
A road that bends, without an end,
With every star, my thoughts ascend.

The whispers of the night take flight,
They weave my hopes with soft moonlight.
Through fields of wonder, I shall roam,
This unseen trail, forever home.

Each step I take, a heartbeat shown,
A melody of seeds I've sown.
The future glows on airy wings,
In every breath, a promise sings.

The trail may hide in dark's embrace,
Yet dreams shine bright, and I find grace.
Through unseen paths, my soul will soar,
To realms where dreams lead evermore.

Shadows in the Thicket

Among the trees where shadows play,
I find my heart, I lose my way.
The thicket holds its secrets tight,
In whispers wrapped, both soft and light.

The rustling leaves, a distant call,
Of stories whispered, one and all.
In tangled roots, my thoughts entwine,
With nature's pulse, a sacred sign.

I breathe the earth, so rich and deep,
In shadows where the giants sleep.
Here in the thicket, lost yet found,
A refuge where my dreams abound.

With every step, the light does dance,
In shadowed pathways, I find chance.
A journey through the wild and free,
In thicket shadows, I shall see.